Cottage Gardens

Cottage Gardens

WEIDENFELD AND NICOLSON

LONDON

INTRODUCTION

*I*nvited to imagine the perfect cottage, most people would picture not only its size, what it was built with, and the colour of its front door, but – perhaps most importantly – its small but perfectly formed garden. There might be a rose or honeysuckle planted by the door, a topiary peacock standing sentinel at the gate, a short grassy, paved or gravel path, perhaps a venerable apple tree laden with blossom or rosy fruit. Certainly on a warm summer's day there would be the hum of bees busily at work, butterflies flitting from flower to flower and a thrush or blackbird poised on an overhanging branch. A strong scent might come from lavender, rose-

mary, lilies or sweet-smelling stocks; colour from brilliant blue cornflowers or delphiniums, poppies of exotic origin, rainbow-hued pelargoniums and pansies, soft old-fashioned roses or rampant clematis entwined round a well-placed pillar or rustic arch.

Whatever the reality, most people have as strong a view of their ideal cottage garden as they do of the house. Not all have the same features, but all do have something in common: a characteristic that could perhaps be defined as abundance. The typical cottage garden is always filled to overflowing with a mass of plants, usually very colourful and frequently in a jumble. The lettuces and cabbages may be in neat rows, but the traditional cottage garden plants are least happy confined to their prescribed plot; they jostle for space, fill their beds to capacity and gracefully spill over the edges.

The cottage gardener has myriad choices to make, all of them pleasurable. The vignettes within this little book represent at least one aspect of someone's ideal cottage garden – it is hoped that they will provide the inspiration for many more.

NORFOLK

*S*URROUNDING a cottage typical of the flint-and-brick houses in East Anglia are large groups of red valerian, a plant that seeds itself readily. Their colour beautifully complements the roof tiles and bricks of the cottage. It is also available in pink and white forms, though the white is harder to find.

SUFFOLK

L AVENDER is one of the principal ingredients of the traditional English cottage garden, like this one in Lavenham. Grown mainly for its heady fragrance and attractive colour, it is commonly used in pot pourri and as an oil. Bees that feed on lavender produce a delicious, distinctively flavoured honey.

SURREY

*T*HE yellow-flowered loosestrife – *Lysima-chia punctata* – makes a strong impact in this garden in Shamley Green. Its height makes it a good choice for a bed sited a short distance from the house. The plant spreads rapidly and is particularly fond of boggy ground.

SOMERSET

*I*N East Coker, the village in which T. S. Eliot was born and which he immortalized in his *Four Quartets*, is a thatched cottage of fourteenth-century origin. The path is lined with hollyhocks, which can grow to a height of eight feet.

———•·•·•———

SUFFOLK

*B*ESIDE a sixteenth-century thatched cottage lies a small herb garden, intricately arranged into a centre bed holding six types of sage, six marjorams, six rosemaries and twenty-five creeping thymes. Surrounding borders feature everything from jasmine to *Akebia quinata* – altogether some two hundred different herbs.

CORNWALL

*T*HE dense planting and juxtaposition of strong colours in this border are found in cottage gardens all over the country. The dusky mauve cranesbill is a particular favourite, divides easily and is not difficult to grow.

HAMPSHIRE

*T*HE white wicket gate, gravel path, bamboo wigwam and spots of colour are typical of the English cottage garden. The magnificent topiary peacock coupled with a 'wedding cake' is one of four examples in Basing said to date to the seventeenth century.

NORFOLK

*F*OXGLOVE, yellow
alchemilla and red valer-
ian, rose, lilies, hollyhocks
and honeysuckle – all these
mingle in a cottage garden
in Wiveton. They grow to-
gether, as if by accident,
which produces a gorgeous
palette of colour.

SUFFOLK

*A*s if giving directions, this group of *Lilium regale* fronting a row of beans bears testimony to all that has been written in praise of the lily. In the quiet of early morning or after rain, its entrancing scent is capable of reviving the most weary soul.

KENT

*S*UBTLE colours make up a unique composition in a garden that was planted by a watercolourist many decades ago. Though the garden is now maintained by his son, the beauty in the artful combination of hues and tints of the plants remains.

NORFOLK

*T*HE garden of a seven-
teenth-century mill con-
tains uncountable surprises: a
niche surrounded by *Dac-
tylorrhiza elata* – a member
of the orchid family – can-
delabra primulas, ligularia
and hosta holds a statue of
St Fiacre, a patron saint of
gardeners.

WILTSHIRE

A COTTAGE in the village of Great Bed-wyn is home to a large garden, part of which is devoted to herbs. Edged in box and separated into two sections, the various herbs – with standard rose plants in the centre – are alternated in squares with gravel, creating a chequerboard pattern.

EAST SUSSEX

$\mathcal{S}$ TANDING proudly in front of a cottage
in Wartling Hill, this ancient yew tree has
witnessed the village life of many generations.
Stories about the yew tree have circulated for
centuries, from its function as a symbol of the
afterlife in pagan rituals to Shakepeare's noting
of its poisonous berries.

CORNWALL

*E*NCOUNTERED by the Spaniards in the New World, the California poppy – *Eschscholzia* – once blanketed regions of America. Imported into the English cottage garden, it has long been enjoyed for its extended flowering period.

NORFOLK

*T*HE sensibility of a sculptor pervades this intriguing garden. The owner used the contours of plants to create unexpected group-ings. The many shades of green, including the lime-green flowers of the annual nicotiana, help establish an air of tranquillity.

KENT

— ◆ —

A DIVERSE range of plants border this
fifteenth-century half-timbered cottage
in Wittersham. The beautiful plate-size leaves
of the hostas are a tribute to the gardener's
success in slug control. The hanging baskets
on either side of the honeysuckle have been
planted in complementary colours.

———◆———

Surrey

*D*ELPHINIUMS come in many shades of blue and pink, from white to almost black. Here their strong vertical thrust out of the dense undergrowth echoes the slats of the wooden fence edging the garden.

———•◦•◦•———

DORSET

*T*HE topiary lining the front path of this cottage and clipped in a spiral shape provides a geometric counterpoint to the blocked forms on the opposite side of the walk.

CORNWALL

*B*RUSHED by the Gulf Stream, the comparatively warm climate of England's southwest coast provides ideal growing conditions for many native plants and more fertile ground for less hardy visitors. In this garden, foxgloves, including the indigenous *Digitalis purpurea*, battle for space with spurge, poppies and daisies.

SUFFOLK

*T*HE Gothic-style woodwork is just one element of the enticing garden of this seventeenth-century cottage. The grassy path, unkempt topiary, rose-festooned rustic arch and the ivy and honeysuckle growing by the door all contribute to the timeless character of this garden.

KENT

*T*HIS outstanding herb garden contains every herb mentioned in Shakepeare's plays. There are more than fifty varieties here, from wild thyme and lovage to lemon balm and Ophelia's rosemary.

HEREFORDSHIRE

*D*OMINATING the garden of a sixteenth-century thatched cottage in Ayhill are two large topiary whose mushroom shape reflects the soft curve of the thatched roof and the mature mounds of the plants in the herbaceous border beneath them.

Surrey

*A*MBER heleniums and blue globe thistle
are good plants to attract bees, welcomed
by gardeners for their help in pollinating, and of
course for their honey by those who have hives.

CORNWALL

*H*UDDLED around the lattice-windowed door of an eighteenth-century house are a pleasing combination of scented plants. A *Magnolia sieboldii*, with its fresh fragrance, arcs over the spicy *Geranium macrorrhizum* and pineapple mint and fern, while to the right the sharp swords of iris provide a pleasing constrast of leaf shape.

ACKNOWLEDGEMENTS

Copyright © George Weidenfeld and Nicolson 1994

First published in Great Britain in 1994 by George Weidenfeld and Nicolson Ltd
Orion House, 5 Upper St Martin's Lane, London WC2H 9EA

British Library Cataloguing-in-Publication Data
A catalogue record for this book is available from the British Library

Cover and series design by Peter Bridgewater/Bridgewater Book Company
Series Editor: Lucas Dietrich

Photographs
*Clay Perry: half-title, title, pages 3, 7, 9, 11, 13, 17, 21, 23, 25, 27, 31, 33, 35, 37,
39, 43, 45, 51, 53; Clive Boursnell: 15, 29, 47; George Wright: 19, 41, 49*